The Sayings of Robert Burns

The Sayings of

ROBERT
BURNS

edited by

Robert Pearce

DUCKWORTH

First published in 1998 by
Gerald Duckworth & Co. Ltd.
61 Frith Street, London W1V 5TA
Tel: 0171 434 4242
Fax: 0171 434 4420
Email: duckworth-publishers.co.uk

Introduction and editorial arrangement
© 1998 by Robert Pearce

A catalogue record for this book is available
from the British Library

ISBN 0 7156 2838 0

Typeset by Ray Davies
Printed in Great Britain by
Redwood Books Ltd, Trowbridge

Contents

Introduction

Robert Burns was born in a two-roomed cottage ('an auld clay biggin') in Alloway, Ayrshire, on 25 January 1759, a date which – with the annual celebration of Burns Night in Scotland and indeed throughout the world – must now rank as the second most famous birthday in the history of mankind. He was the eldest of the seven children born to a struggling tenant farmer and his wife, William and Agnes Burness. Arduous farm work and under-nourishment probably harmed Robert's health, and he received relatively little formal schooling; but in fact he had a remarkably good education. His father encouraged him to read widely and he was well versed by one of his mother's friends, whom he described as 'remarkable for her ignorance, credulity and superstition', in Scottish folk songs and legends. He began composing poems in the 1770s.

Writing was, in part, consolation for failure as a farmer. When his father died in 1784, Robert and his brother Gilbert rented Mossgiel Farm, near Mauchline, but the venture was not a success. A farm in Ellisland, leased later in the decade, proved similarly unproductive. He was forced to take a position in the Excise Service in Dumfries from 1789 but was rarely free of money troubles. Poetry was a refuge also from a tempestuous love life. He undoubtedly had an eye for 'rapture-giving woman'. 'My heart,' he wrote, 'was completely tinder, and was eternally lighted up by some Goddess or other.' (Or, as a friend wrote, no one was 'a greater fool' than Robbie Burns where women were concerned.)

Burns's first illegitimate child was born on 22 May 1785, to Elizabeth Paton, a servant who had attended his father's last illness; and in the same year he fell in love with Jean Armour, the daughter of a Mauchline master mason. Several times the couple were called to the local kirk to receive public rebuke for their behaviour, but when Jean became pregnant her father refused to allow them to marry. James Armour sent his daughter to relatives in Paisley. Burns planned to emigrate to the West Indies and was deterred only by the publication of his *Poems, Chiefly in the Scottish Dialect* in 1786. Drawing inspiration from the works of Robert Ferguson and Allan Ramsay, it was a landmark in Scottish literature. Its first edition of six hundred copies made him a profit of only twenty pounds, but he determined to stay in Scotland and publish more work. He moved to Edinburgh, where for a time he was lionised – and patronised – by literary society as a Ploughman Poet, pouring out the wild effusions of his heart. He was indeed a fine talker – unsurpassed, it was said, in the 'spontaneous eloquence of social argument, or the unstudied poignancy of brilliant repartee'. Sir Walter Scott recalled that his eye 'literally glowed when he spoke with feeling or interest. I never saw another such eye in a human head, though I have seen the most distinguished men in my time'. Yet Burns soon tired of such an artificial role and, after issuing a more lucrative second edition of his poems, embarked on a tour of the country, collecting and preserving traditional Scots ballads. After several more affairs, he married Jean Armour, who had borne him twins. She tolerated her temperamental husband with great understanding, even raising one of his illegitimate daughters. 'Our Robbie,' she commented philosophically, 'should have had twa wives.' There were indeed several Juliets to this Romeo.

Burns is sometimes quite unfairly dismissed as a drunken rake. It has been said that he fathered around 70 children, drank himself to death and, a pauper, was found frozen in the snow. The historical record, however, is more prosaic. His role as a ladies' man is remarkably well-documented but in fact was not particularly unusual. Certainly arraignment before the

Calvinists at the Kirk Session was by no means a rare occurrence in the second half of the eighteenth century. In addition, his drinking excesses were exaggerated by his enemies. His praise of 'John Barleycorn' is, at times, so complete and unrestrained as to be positively romantic. This was not the testimony of an alcoholic: there is no evidence that Burns ever became sick and tired of being sick and tired. He himself wrote that a man 'perpetually in the paroxysms and fevers of inebriety is like a half-drowned, stupid wretch condemned to labour unceasingly in water, but a now-and-then tribute to Bacchus is like the cold bath – bracing and invigorating.' Occasional drinking, he insisted, 'defecates the standing pool of thought'. Furthermore, although at his death he left a sizable sum, for most of his life he simply did not have the money to over-indulge. Finally, his prodigious output and the sheer artistry of such poems as 'Scotch Drink' give the lie to the myth of the whisky-sodden bard. It is also revealing that the man reputed to have been frozen to death died, from rheumatic fever, on 21 July 1796.

More remarkable than his private life were his radical politics. His experience of poverty gave him a profound sympathy with the exploited and the down-trodden and a fierce contempt for his 'superiors' who consumed without producing. As a result, he found it very difficult to attract a patron, but his verse benefited enormously. His was not the smouldering envy of the peasant but the proud, spirited and generous anger of the righteous. His withering satire reveals a true opponent of cant, hypocrisy and injustice, and much of his best poetry is politically subversive. Brotherhood, he knew, demands equality. His works have an honoured place in the 'psalmody of radicalism', alongside those of Tom Paine, William Cobbett and the young William Wordsworth. In 1919 the socialist Karl Liebknecht was shot in Germany; in his pocket was a translation of the lines 'That man to man, the world o'er, Shall brothers be for a' that.'

Yet what stands out about Burns is not the singleness but the breadth of his vision. Thomas Carlyle called him 'the largest soul of all the British lands' and Byron judged that he had an 'antithetical mind', combining delicacy and coarseness, sentiment and sensuality, dirt and deity, 'all mixed up in that one compound of inspired clay'. A man of intellectual distinction and of complex character, his poems sing the full range of human emotions. At times he even seems contradictory. The Dionysian reveller is also, occasionally, the stern-eyed puritan. (In him Wisdom and Folly meet, mix and unite; Virtue and Vice blend their black and their white.) There's bawdiness and exquisite, sad tenderness. But such inconsistency mirrors the nature of life itself, whose moods Burns portrayed so memorably. Hence he could appeal equally to men as different in temperament as Wordsworth and, from a later generation, D.H. Lawrence. Burns knew what Lawrence called 'the kissing and the horrid strife'; but not for him 'the dead vanity of knowing better', 'the blank cold comfort of superiority' or the 'silly conceit of being immune'.

The last five years of his life were devoted to collecting traditional ballads. He collected over 300 songs, or fragments, thus preserving an important aspect of Scots heritage. He first heard 'Auld Lang Syne' being sung by an old man. 'Light be the turf on the breast of the heaven-inspired Poet who composed this glorious fragment.' Yet Burns did more than merely record: he added his own touch of genius, transforming the temporal into the immortal, so that we may judge that he too was inspired.

At the age of 36 Burns wrote that he was feeling 'the rigid fibre & stiffening joints of Old Age coming fast o'er my bones'. The following year he died. Here was 'a devilish change indeed'. Yet on the morning of the funeral his wife Jean gave birth to another son – a fitting memorial for a man who so valued life and love.

Samuel Brydges wrote that Burns 'did not merely appear to be a poet at casual intervals; but at every moment a poetical enthusiasm seemed to beat in his veins, and he lived all his days the inward if not the outward life of a poet.' His worth was widely recognised after his death. His poems have been translated into 40 different languages, and it has even been computed that an average of ten new editions of his works have appeared every year since 1786. In addition, almost a thousand volumes of biography have been written about him. Justifiably do Scots feel a special pride in Burns, as he was proud of his nation; but Scotland's greatest poet is also an important figure in world literature. As Emerson said, the works of Robert Burns 'are the property and solace of mankind'. He was a poet for all seasons. The Scots bard is also the bard, and benefactor, of humanity.

R.D.P.

Sources

Quotations are taken from the Kilmarnock (1786) and Edinburgh (1787) editions and from James Currie, *The Complete Works of Robert Burns with an Account of his Life* (Milner and Sowerby, London, 1800).

Logic & Perception

O wad some Power the giftie gie us
To see oursels as ithers see us!

'To a Louse'

Facts are chiels that winna ding,
And downa be disputed.

'A Dream'

The passing moment's all we rest on!

'Sketch – New Year's Day'

Good Lord, what is Man! for as simple as he looks,
Do but try to develop his hooks and his crooks;
With his depths and his shallows, his good and his evil,
All in all he's a problem must puzzle the devil.

'Sketch in Verse'

Gin a body meet a body
Coming through the rye;
Gin a body kiss a body,
Need a body cry?

'Coming through the Rye'

Why is outlandish stuff sae meikle courted?
Does nonsense mend, like brandy, when imported?

'Scots Prologue for Mr Sutherland'

The lily's hue, the rose's dye,
The kindling lustre of an eye;
Who but knows their magic sway?
Who but knows they all decay?

'My Peggy's Charms'

Beauty, how frail and how fleeting!
The bloom of a fine summer's day!

'Phillis the Queen o' the Fair'

Himself

For me! sae laigh I need na bow,
For, Lord be thankit, I can plough.   'A Dedication'

God have mercy on me! a poor damned incautious,
duped, unfortunate fool! The sport, the miserable victim,
of rebellious pride, hypocondriac imagination, agonizing
sensibility, and bedlam passions!

Letter to Peggy, January 1788

For my own part I never had the least thought or
inclination of turning Poet till I got once heartily in love,
and then Rhyme and Song were, in a manner, the
spontaneous language of my heart.   *Journal*, August 1793

I sometimes think the character of a certain great man I
have read of somewhere is very much à-propos to
myself – that he was a compound of great talents and
great folly.   *Ibid.*

He who of Rankine sang, lies stiff and dead,
And a green grassy hillock hides his head;
Alas! alas! a devilish change indeed.

'Lines on the Author's Death'

Some of our folk … have conceived a prejudice against
me as being a drunken dissipated character. I might be
all this, you know, and yet be an honest fellow, but you
know that I am an honest fellow and am nothing of this.

Letter to Samuel Clarke, n.d.

God knows I am no saint; I have a whole host of follies
and sins to answer for; but if I could, and I believe I do it
as far as I can, I would wipe away all tears from all eyes.

Letter to Mr Hill, 2 March 1790

I do now want to be independent that I may sin, but I do
want to be independent in my sinning.

Letter to Mr Cunningham, 11 June 1791

Hypocrisy

O ye wha are sae guid yoursel',
   Sae pious and sae holy,
Ye've nought to do but mark and tell
   Your neibours' faults and folly!

'Address to an Unco Guid'

Stretch a point to catch a plack;
Abuse a brother to his back;
Steal thro' the winnock frae a whore,
But point the rake that taks the door;
Be to the poor like onie whunstane,
And haud their noses to the grunstane;
Ply ev'ry legal art of thieving;
No matter – stick to sound believing.

'A Dedication'

Learn three-mile prayers, an' half-mile graces,
Wi' well-spread looves, an' lang, wry faces;
Grunt up a solemn, lengthened groan,
And damn a' parties but your own;
I'll warrant, then we're nae deceiver,
A steady, sturdy, staunch believer.

Ibid.

I bless and praise Thy matchless might,
When thousands Thou has left in night,
That I am here afore Thy sight,
   For gifts an' grace
A burning and a shining light
   To a' this place.

'Holy Willie's Prayer'

But yet, O Lord! confess I must,
At times I'm fashed wi' fleshly lust.

Ibid.

Lord, in Thy day o' vengeance try him,
Lord, visit them wha did employ him,
And pass not in Thy mercy by them,
    Nor hear their prayer,
But for Thy people's sake destroy them,
    An' dinna spare.

Ibid.

But, Lord, remember me an' mine
Wi' mercies temporal and divine,
That I for grace an' gear may shine,
    Excelled by nane,
And a' the glory shall be thine,
    Amen, Amen!   *Ibid.*

Life is all a variorum,
    We regard not how it goes;
Let them cant about decorum,
    Who have character to lose.

'The Jolly Beggars'

Ye hypocrites! are these your pranks?
To murder men and give God thanks!
Desist, for shame! – proceed no further;
God won't accept your thanks for MURTHER!

'Thanksgiving for a National Victory'

They take religion in their mouth;
They talk o' mercy, grace an' truth,
For what? – to gie their malice skouth
    On some puir wight,
An' hunt him down, owre right and ruth,
    To ruin straight.

'Epistle to the Rev. John McMath'

God knows, I'm no the thing I should be,
Nor am I even the thing I could be,
But twenty times I rather would be,
    An atheist clean,
Than under gospel colours hid be,
    Just for a screen.

Ibid.

The more 'tis a truth, sir, the more 'tis a libel!

'The Libeller's Self-Reproof'

Here's freedom to them that wad read,
    Here's freedom to them that wad write,
There's nane ever feared that the truth should be
    heard,
    But them whom the truth would indite.

'Here's a Health to Them That's Awa''

Conceal yoursel' as weel's ye can
Frae critical dissection;
But keek thro' ev'ry other man,
Wi' sharpened, sly inspection.

'Epistle to a Young Friend'

The thundering bully may rage,
    And swagger and swear like a heathen;
But collar him fast, I'll engage
    You'll find that his courage is – naething.

'Stanzas on Naething'

I never had frien's well stockit in means,
    To leave me a hundred or twa, man;
Nae well-tochered aunts, to wait on their drants,
    And wish them in hell for it a', man.

'The Ronalds of the Bennals'

With your honours, as with a certain king,
    In your servants this is striking,
The more incapacity they bring,
    The more they're to your liking.

'The Dean of Faculty'

Men display to congregations wide
Devotion's ev'ry grace, except the heart.

'The Cotter's Saturday Night'

Alcohol

Ilka man that's drunk's a lord.

'Gudewife, Count the Lawin'

The clachan yill had made me canty,
I was na fou, but just had plenty.

'Death and Doctor Holbrook'

Go, find an honest fellow,
    Good claret set before thee,
Hold on till thou art mellow,
    And then to bed in glory.

'Deluded Swain, The Pleasure'

Let other poets raise a fracas
'Bout vines, and wines, an' drunken Bacchus,
An' crabbit names 'an stories wrack us,
    An' grate our lug:
I sing the juice Scotch bear can make us,
    In glass or jug.

'Scotch Drink'

Leeze me on thee, John Barlaycorn,
    Thou king o' grain.   *Ibid.*

Gie him strong drink until he wink,
    That's sinking in despair;
An' liquor guid to fire his bluid,
    That's prest wi' grief and care.

                                        Ibid.

Food fills the wame, an' keeps us livin;
Tho' life's a gift no worth receivin,
When heavy-dragged wi' pine an grievin;
    But oiled by thee,
The wheels o' life gae down-hill, scrievin,
    Wi' rattlin glee.   *Ibid.*

Thou clears the head o' doited Lear;
Thou cheers the heart o' drooping Care;
Thou strings the nerves o' Labour sair
   At's weary toil;
Thou even brightens dark Despair
   Wi' gloomy smile.   *Ibid.*

When neighbors anger at a plea,
An' just as wud as wud can be,
How easy can the barley brie
   Cement the quarrel!
It's aye the cheapeast lawyer's fee,
   To taste the barrel.   *Ibid.*

O whisky! soul o' plays and pranks!
Accept a bardie's gratefu' thanks!
When wanting thee, what tuneless cranks
   Are my poor verses!   *Ibid.*

Fortune! if thou'll but gie me still
Hale breeks, a scone, an' whisky gill,
An' rowth o' rhyme to rave at will,
   Tak' a' the rest,
An' deal't about as thy blind skill
   Directs thee best.   *Ibid.*

There's naething like the honest nappy;
Whare'll ye e'er see men sae happy,
Or women sonsie, saft an' sappy,
   'Tween morn and morn,
As them wha like to taste the drappie,
   In glass or horn?   'Epistle to John Goldie'

Leeze me on drink! it gies us mair
   Then either school or college;
It kindles wit, it waukens lear,
   It pangs us fou o' knowledge:
Be't whisky-gill or penny wheep,
   Or any stronger potion,
It never fails, on drinkin deep,
   To kittle up our notion,
By night or day.   'The Holy Fair'

There's some are fou o' love divine;
   There's some are fou o' brandy;
An' mony jobs that day begin,
   May end in houghmagandie.

Ibid.

Freedom and Whisky gang thegither!
       'The Author's Earnest Cry and Prayer'

Sages their solemn een may steek,
An' raise a philosophic reek,
An' physically causes seek
   In clime an' season;
But tell me whisky's name in Greek,
   I'll tell the reason.

Ibid.

Inspiring bold John Barleycorn!
What dangers thou canst make us scorn!
Wi' tipenny, we fear nae evil;
Wi' usquabae, we'll face the devil!

'Tam O'Shanter'

Kings may be blest, but Tam was glorious,
O'er a' the ills o' life victorious!

Ibid.

Whene'er to Drink you are inclined,
Or Cutty Sarks rin in your mind,
Think ye may buy the joys o'er dear;
Remember Tam O'Shanter's mare.

Ibid.

Strong ale was ablution,
Small beer persecution,
   A dram was momento mori;
But a full-flowing bowl
Was the saving his soul,
   And port was celestial glory.

'Epitaph on John Dove, Innkeeper'

Here's a bottle and an honest friend!
    What wad ye wish for mair, man?
Wha kens, before his life may end,
    What his share may be o' care, man?
                                                    'A Bottle and a Friend'

No churchman am I for to rail and to write,
No stateman or soldier to plot or to fight,
No sly man of business contriving a snare,
For a big-belly'd bottle's the whole of my care.
                                                    'No Churchman am I'

John Barleycorn was a hero bold,
    Of noble enterprise;
For if you do but taste his blood,
    'Twill make your courage rise.
'Twill make a man forget his woe;
    'Twill heighten all his joy;
'Twill make the widow's heart to sing,
    'Tho' the tear were in her eye.
Then let us toast John Barleycorn,
    Each man a glass in hand;
And may his great posterity
    Ne'er fail in old Scotland!
                                                    'John Barleycorn: A Ballad'

Satan, I fear thy sooty claws,
    I hate thy brunstane stink,
And aye I curse the luckless cause –
    The wicked soup o' drink.
                                                    'To William Stewart'

Gude ale keeps the heart aboon!
                                                    'Gude Ale'

My coggie is a haly pool
That heals the wounds o' care and dool;
And Pleasure is a wanton trout,
An ye drink it a', ye'll find him out.
                                                    'Gudewife, Count the Lawin'

Nature

I'm truly sorry man's dominion
Has broken Nature's social union.

'To a Mouse'

Nature's law,
That man was made to mourn.

'Man was Made to Mourn'

Nature's charms, the hills and woods,
The sweeping vales, and foaming floods,
   Are free alike to all.

'Epistle to David, a Brother Poet'

Inhuman man! curse on thy barb'rous art,
   And blasted be thy murder-aiming eye;
   May never pity soothe thee with a sigh,
Nor ever pleasure glad thy cruel heart!

'The Wounded Hare'

O Nature! a' thy shews and forms
To feeling, pensive hearts she charms!
Whether the summer kindly warms,
   Wi' life an' light;
Or winter howls, in gusty storms,
   The lang, dark night!

'Epistle to William Simson'

Man, your proud usurping foe,
Would be lord of all below:
Plumes himself in freedom's pride,
Tyrant stern to all beside.

'On Scaring some Water-Fowl'

Nature's gifts to all are free.

Ibid.

The eagle, from the cliffy brow,
Marking you his prey below,
In his breast no pity dwells,
Strong necessity compels:
But Man, to whom alone is given
A ray direct from pitying Heaven,
Glories in his heart humane –
And creatures for his pleasures slain!

Ibid.

For thus the royal mandate ran,
When first the human race began;
'The social, friendly, honest man,
    Whate'er he be –
'Tis *he* fulfils great Nature's plan,
    And none but he.'

'Second Epistle to J. Lapraik'

That auld capricious carlin, Nature.

'Epistle to James Smith'

Nature is adverse to a cripple's rest.

'Second Epistle to Robert Graham'

Auld Nature swears, the lovely dears
    Her noblest work she classes, O:
Her prentice han' she tried on man,
    An' then she made the lasses, O.

'Green Grow the Rashes'

My heart's in the Highlands, my heart is not here,
My heart's in the Highlands, a-chasing the deer;
A-chasing the wild-deer, and following the roe,
My heart's in the Highlands wherever I go.

'My Heart's in the Highlands'

Your Beauty's a flower, in the morning that blows,
And withers the faster, the faster it grows:
But the rapturous charm o' the bonie greed knowes,
Ilk spring they're new deckit wi' bonie white
yowes.

'A Lass Wi' A Tocher'

Mark the winds, and mark the skies,
  Ocean's ebb and ocean's flow;
Sun and moon but set to rise;
  Round and round the seasons go.
Why then ask of silly man
To oppose great Nature's plan?
We'll be content while we can –
  You can be no more, you know.

'Inconstancy in Love'

Let others love the city,
  And gaudy show, at sunny noon;
Gie me the lonely valley,
  The dewy eve, the rising moon.

'Sae Flaxen were her Ringlets'

Great Nature spoke, with air benign;
  'Go on, ye human race;
This lower world I you resign;
  Be fruitful and increase.
The liquid fire of strong desire,
  I've poured it in each bosom;
Here on this hand does Mankind stand,
  And there is Beauty's blossom!'

'Nature's Law'

The voice of Nature loudly cries,
And many a message from the skies,
That something in us never dies.

'New Year's Day'

When Nature her great masterpiece designed,
And framed her last, best work, the human mind,
Her eye intent on all the wondrous plan,
She formed of various stuff the various Man.

'To Robert Graham'

Religion & Morality

They never sought in vain that sought the Lord aright!

'The Cotter's Saturday Night'

The honest heart that's free frae a'
   Intended fraud or guile,
However Fortune kicks the ba',
   Has aye some cause to smile.

'Epistle to Davie, Brother Poet'

Deep this truth impressed my mind –
   Thro' all His work abroad,
The heart benevolent and kind
   The most resembles God.

'A Winter Night'

Say, to be just, and kind, and wise –
There solid self-enjoyment lies;
That foolish, selfish, faithless ways
Lead to be wretched, vile, and base.

'Written in Friars' Carse Hermitage'

How Wisdom and Folly meet, mix, and unite,
How Virtue and Vice blend their black and their white,
How Genius, th' illustrious father of fiction,
Confounds rule and law, reconciles contradiction,
I sing.   'Sketch in Verse'

Preserve the dignity of Man,
   With soul erect;
And trust the Universal Plan
   Will all protect.

'The Vision'

But yet the light that led astray
Was light from Heaven.

Ibid.

All villain as I am – a damned wretch,
A hardened, stubborn, unrepenting sinner –
Still my heart melts at human wretchedness,
And with sincere tho' unavailing sighs
I view the helpless children of distress.
With tears indignant I behold the oppressor
Rejoicing in the honest man's destruction,
Whose unsubmitting heart was all his crime.

'Tragic Fragment'

All hail, Religion! maid divine!
Pardon a muse sae mean as mine,
Who in her rough imperfect line
    Thus daurs to name thee;
To stigmatise false friends of thine
    Can ne'er defame thee.

'Epistle to the Rev. John McMath'

An honest man may like a glass,
An honest man may like a lass,
But mean revenge and malice fause
    He'll still disdain.

Ibid.

Some, lucky, find a flow'ry spot,
For which they never toiled nor swat;
They drink the sweet and eat the fat,
    But care or pain;
And haply eye the barren hut
    With high disdain.

'Epistle to James Smith'

That he's the poor man's friend in need,
The gentleman in word and deed,
It's not thro' terror of damnation,
It's just a carnal inclination.

'A Dedication'

Ye'll get the best o' moral works,
'Mang black Gentoos, and pagan Turks,
Or hunters wild on Ponotaxi,
Wha never heard of orthodoxy.   *Ibid.*

Then at the balance let's be mute,
    We never can adjust it;
What's done we partly may compute,
    But know not what's resisted.

'Address to an Unco Guid'

My son, these maxims make a rule,
    And lump them ay thegither:
The Rigid Righteous is a fool,
    The Rigid Wise anither;
The cleanest corn that e'er was dight
    May hae some pyles o' chaff in;
So ne'er a fellow-creature slight
    For random fits o' daffin.   *Ibid.*

Life is not worth having with all it can give –
For something beyond it poor man sure must live.

'The Fall of the Leaf'

What are Priests (those seeming godly wise-men,)
What are they, pray, but Spiritual Excisemen!

'Kirk and State Excisemen'

You shouldna paint at angels, man,
    But try and paint the devil.
To paint an Angel's kittle wark,
    Wi' Nick there's little danger:
You'll easy draw a lang-kent face,
    But no sae weel a stranger.

'Epigram Addressed to an Artist'

On ev'ry hand it will allowed be,
He's just – nae better than he should be.

'A Dedication to Gavin Hamilton'

Cease ye prudes, your envious railing!

'Picture of the Celebrated Miss Burns'

Ask why God made the gem so small,
    And why so huge the granite? –
Because God meant mankind should set
    That higher value on it.   'Epigram on Miss Davies'

The deities that I adore
    Are social Peace and Plenty;
I'm better pleased to make one more,
    Than by the death of twenty.

'I Murder Hate'

Some sairie comfort at the last,
    When a' thir days are done, man,
My pains o' hell on earth is past,
    I'm sure o' bliss aboon, man.

'O Aye My Wife She Dang Me'

Here lies Boghead among the dead
    In hopes to get salvation;
But if such as he in Heav'n may be,
    Then welcome, hail! damnation.

'Epitaph on James Grieve'

What man could esteem, or what woman could love,
    Was he who lies under this sod:
If such Thou refusest admission above,
    Then whom wilt Thou favour, Good God?

'Epitaph on Robert Muir'

Poor Centum-per-Centum may fast,
    And grumble his hurdies their claithing,
He'll find, when the balance is cast,
    He's gane to the devil for – naething.

'Stanzas on Naething'

The priest anathèmas may threat –
    Predicament, sir, that we're baith in;
But when honour's reveillé is beat,
    The holy artillery's – naething.   *Ibid.*

I never barked when out of season,
    I never bit without a reason;
I ne'er insulted weaker brother,
    Nor wronged by force or fraud another.
We brutes are placed a rank below;
    Happy for a man could he say so.

'On a Dog of Lord Eglinton's'

Firm as a creed, Sirs, 'tis my fixed belief,
That Misery's another word for Grief.

'Address'

The great Creator to revere,
    Must sure become the creature;
But still the preaching cant forbear,
    And ev'n the rigid feature:
Yet ne'er with wits profane to range,
    Be complaisance extended;
An atheist-laugh's a poor exchange
    For Deity offended.

'Epistle to a Young Friend'

All I want (O do Thou grant
    This one request of mine!):
Since to enjoy Thou dost deny,
    Assist me to resign.

'Winter: A Dirge'

Thou know'st that Thou hast formed me
    With passions wild and strong;
And list'ning to their twitching voice
    Has often led me wrong.

'A Prayer in the Prospect of Death'

No man can say in what degree any other person,
besides himself, can be, with strict justice, called *wicked*.

Journal, March 1794

Whatever mitigates the woes, or increases the happiness
of others, this is my criterion of goodness; and whatever
injures society, or any individual in it, this is my measure
of iniquity.

Letter to Mrs Dunlop, 21 June 1789

Of all Nonsense, Religious Nonsense is the most
nonsensical.

Letter to Mr Cunningham, 10 September 1792

Politics

Princes and lords are but the breath of kings.

'The Cotter's Saturday Night'

Why has man the will and power
  To make his fellows mourn?

'Man was Made to Mourn'

Scots, wha hae wi' Wallace bled,
Scots, wham Bruce has aften led,
Welcome to your glory bed
  Or to victorie.

'Scota Wha Hae'

Lay the proud usurpers low!
Tyrants fall in every foe!
Liberty's in every blow! –
  Let us do or die!   *Ibid.*

A fig for those by law protected!
  Liberty's a glorious feast!
Courts for cowards were erected,
  Churches built to please the priest.

'The Jolly Beggars'

But loyalty – truce! We're on dangerous ground;
Who knows how the fashions may alter?
The doctrine, to-day, that is loyally sound,
To-morrow may bring us a halter!

'Address to Wm. Tytler, Esq'

The English steel we could disdain,
  Secure in valour's station;
But English gold has been our bane –
  Such a parcel of rogues in a nation!

'Such a Parcel of Rogues'

In the field of proud honour, our swords in our hands,
    Our king and our country to save;
While victory shines on Life's last ebbing sands, –
    O who would not die with the brave?

                         'The Song of Death'

Were this the charter of our state,
'On pain o' hell be rich an' great,'
Damnation then would be our fate,
    Beyone remead;
But, thanks to heaven, that's no the gate
    We learn our creed.

                  'Second Epistle to J. Lapraik'

I muckle doubt, my sire,
Ye've trusted ministration
To chaps wha in a barn or byre
Wad better filled their station
    Than courts yon day.

                            'A Dream'

While we sing 'God Save the King,'
We'll ne'er forget The People!

          'Does Haughty Gaul Invasion Threat'

The Kirk an' State may join, an' tell
    To do sic things I manna:
The Kirk an' State may gae to hell,
    And I'll gae to my Anna.

               'The Gowden Locks of Anna'

Thus bold, independent, unconquered, and free,
    Her bright course of glory for ever shall run:
For brave Caledonia immortal must be;
    I'll prove it from Euclid as clear as the sun:
Rectangle-triangle, the figure we'll chuse:
    The upright is Chance, and old Time is the base;
But brave Caledonia's the hypothenuse;
    Then, ergo, she'll match them, and match them
        always!

                      'Caledonia: a Ballad'

Grant me, indulgent Heaven, that I may live,
To see the miscreants feel the pains they give;
Deal Freedom's sacred treasures free as air,
Till Slave and Despot be but things that were.

'Lines Inscribed in a Lady's Pocket Almanac'

Edina! Scotia's darling seat!
   All hail thy palaces and tow'rs,
Where ance, beneath a Monarch's feet,
   Sat Litigation's sovereign pow'rs.

'Address to Edinburgh'

In politics if thou would'st mix
   And mean thy fortunes be,
Bear this in mind: Be deaf and blind,
   Let great folks hear and see.

'Politics'

No nation, no station,
   My envy could e'er raise;
A Scot still, but blot still,
   I knew nae higher praise.

'To the Guidwife of Wauchope House'

He gapèd for't, he grapèd for't,
   He fand it was awa, man;
But what his common sense came short,
   He eked out wi' law, man.

'Epigrams'

The injured Stewart line is gone,
A race outlandish fills their throne:
An idiot race, to honour lost –
Who know them best despise them most.

'Written by Somebody on the Window'

It's gude to be merry and wise,
It's gude to be honest and true,
It's gude to support Caledonia's cause
And bide by the bluff and the blue.

'Here's a Health to Them That's Awa' '

Despondency

The best laid schemes o' mice and men
    Gang aft agley,
And lea'e us nought but grief an' pain,
    For promised joy.

'To a Mouse'

Where'er that place be priest ca' hell,
Where a' the tones o' misery yell,
An' rankèd plagues their numbers tell,
    In dreadfu' raw,
Thou, Toothache, surely bear'st the bell,
    Among them a'!

'Address to the Toothache'

O Life! thou art a galling load,
Along a rough, a weary road,
    To wretches such as I!

'Despondency – an Ode'

Still caring, despairing,
    Must be my bitter doom;
My woes here shall close ne'er
    But with the closing tomb.

Ibid.

I, a hope-abandoned wight,
    Unfitted with an aim,
Meet ev'ry sad returning night,
    And joyless morn the same.
You, bustling and justling,
    Forget each grief an' pain;
I, listless yet restless,
    Find ev'ry prospect vain.   *Ibid.*

Hope is born but to expire!

'Elegy on the Death of Sir James Hunter Blair'

Ye banks and braes o' bonie Doon,
    How can ye bloom sae fresh and fair?
How can ye chant, ye little birds,
    And I sae weary fu' o' care!
Thou'll break my heart, thou warbling bird,
    That wantons thro' the flowering thorn:
Thou minds me o' departed joys,
    Departed never to return.

'The Banks o' Doon'

Time cannot aid me, and griefs are immortal,
Nor Hope dare a comfort bestow:
Come then, enamoured and fond of my anguish,
Enjoyment I'll seek in my woe.

'Where Are the Joys I Have Met'

It's hardly in a body's power
To keep, at times, frae being sour,
    To see how things are shared:
How best o' chiels are whiles in want,
While coofs on countless thousands rant,
And ken na how to wair't.

'Epistle to Davie, a Brother Poet'

Here, for my wonted rhyming raptures,
I sit and count my sins by chapters;
For life and spunk like ither Christians,
I've dwindled down to mere existence.

'Epistle to Hugh Parker'

Ae night they're mad wi' drink an' whoring,
Neist day their life is past enduring.

'Twa Dogs'

Still thou are blest, compared wi' me;
The present only toucheth thee:
But och! I backward case my e'e,
    On prospects drear!
An' forward, tho' I canna see,
    I guess an' fear!

'To a Mouse'

When Remembrance wracks the mind,
Pleasures but unveil despair.
                    'Frae the Friends and Land I love'

Endless and deep shall be my grief;
    Nae ray of comfort shall I see,
But this most precious dear belief,
    That thou wilt still remember me!
                    'Behold the Hour'

Fond lovers' parting is sweet, painful pleasure,
    Hope beaming mild on the soft parting hour;
But the dire feeling, O farewell for ever!
    Anguish unmingled, and agony pure!
                    'Thou Gloomy December'

A hungry care is an unco care.
                    'The Country Lass'

Hear me, auld Hangie, for a wee,
An' let poor damnèd bodies be;
I'm sure sma' pleasure it can gie,
    E'en to a deil,
To skelp an' scaud poor dogs like me,
    An' hear us squeel!   'Address to The Deil'

Ev'n thou who mourn'st the Daisy's fate,
That fate is thine – no distant date;
Stern Ruin's plough-share drives elate,
    Full on thy bloom,
Till crushed beneath the furrow's weight,
    Shall be thy doom.
                    'To a Mountain Daisy'

But pleasure are like poppies spread,
You seize the flower, its bloom is shed;
Or like the snow falls in the river,
A moment white – then melts for ever;
Or like the Borealis race,
That flit ere you can point the place;
Or like the Rainbow's lovely form
Evanishing amid the storm.   'Tam O'Shanter'

Veneering oft outshines the solid wood.

'On William Creech'

How long have I lived – how much lived in vain.

'The Fall of the Leaf'

No birds sweetly singing, nor flowers gaily springing,
Can soothe the sad bosom of joyless despair.

'The Chavalier's Lament'

Ah Nick! ah Nick! it is na fair,
First showing us the tempting ware,
Bright wines, and bonie lasses rare,
    To put us daft;
Syne weave, unseen, thy spider snare
    O' hell's damned waft.

'Epistle to Colonel De Peyster'

Come Winter, with thine angry howl,
    And raging, bend the naked tree;
Thy gloom will soothe my cheerless soul,
    When nature all is sad like me!

'Composed in Spring'

Life's to me a weary dream,
A dream of ane that never wauks.

Ibid.

I wander in the ways of men,
Alike unknowing, and unknown.

'Lament for James, Earl of Glencairn'

Man's inhumanity to man
Makes countless thousands mourn!

'Man was Made to Mourn'

Of all the numerous ills that hurt our peace,
That press the soul, or wring the mind with
    anguish,
Beyond comparison the worst are those
By our own folly, or our guilt brought on.

'Remorse – a Fragment'

Remorse is the most painful sentiment that can embitter
the human bosom.   *Journal,* September 1793

In mankind's various paths and ways
There's aye some doytin body strays.

'Election Ballad'

Life, thou soul of every blessing,
Load to misery most distressing,
Gladly how would I resign thee,
And to dark oblivion join thee.

'Raving Winds around her Blowing'

Ye whom sorrow never wounded,
    Ye who never shed a tear,
Care-untroubled, joy-surrounded,
    Gaudy day to you is dear.

'Talk of Him that's Far Awa' '

O how can I be blythe and glad,
    Or how can I gang brisk and braw,
When the bonie lad that I lo'e best
    Is o'er the hills and far awa!

'The Bonie Lad that's Far Awa' '

Dearly bought the hidden treasure
    Finer feelings can bestow:
Chords that vibrate sweetest pleasure
    Thrill the deepest notes of woe.

'Poem on Sensibility'

He's always compleenin frae mornin to eenin,
    He hoasts and he hirples the weary day lang;
He's doylt and he's dozin, his blude it is frozen, –
O dreary's the night wi' a crazy auld man!

'What Can a Young Lassie Do wi' an Auld Man'

While ilka thing in nature join
    Their sorrows to forego,
O why thus all alone are mine
    The weary steps o' woe!

'Now Spring has Clad'

The tempest's howl, it soothes my soul,
    My grief it seems to join;
The leafless trees my fancy please,
    Their fate resembles mine!

'Winter: A Dirge'

Ye dark waste hills, ye brown unsightly plains,
Congenial scenes, ye soothe my mournful strains:
Ye tempests, rage! ye turbid torrents, roll!
Ye suit the joyless tenor of my soul.
Life's social haunts and pleasures I resign;
Be nameless wilds and lonely wanderings mine,
To mourn the woes my country must endure –
That wound degenerate ages cannot cure.

'On the Death of Robert Dundas'

'Tis not the surging billows' roar,
'Tis not the fatal, deadly shore;
Tho' death in ev'ry shape appear,
The wretched have no more to fear:
But round my heart the ties are bound,
The heart transpierced with many a wound;
These bleed afresh, those ties I tear,
To leave the bonie banks of Ayr.

'The Gloomy Night is Gath'ring Fast'

Blow, blow, ye winds, with heavier gust!
And freeze, thou bitter-biting frost!
Descend, ye chilly, smothering snows!
Not all your rage, as now united, shows
    More hard unkindness, unrelenting,
    Vengeful malice, unrepenting,
Than heaven-illumined Man on brother Man bestows!

'A Winter Night'

Now a' is done that men can do,
And a' is done in vain.

'It Was A' for Our Rightfu' King'

In durance vile here must I wake and weep,
And all my frowsy couch in sorrow sleep.

'Epistle from Esopus to Maria'

Education

What's a' your jargon o' your schools –
Your Latin names for horns an' stools?
If honest Nature made you fools,
    What sairs your grammars?
Ye'd better taen up spades and shools,
    Or knappin-hammers.

'Epistle to J. Lapraik'

A set o' dull, conceited hashes
Confuse their brains in college-classes!
They gang in stirks, and come out asses.

Ibid.

Gie me ae spark o' nature's fire,
That's a' the learning I desire;
Then tho' I drudge thro' dub or mire
    At pleugh or cart,
My muse, tho' hamely in attire,
    May touch the heart.

Ibid.

Philosophers have fought and wrangled,
An' meikle Greek and Latin mangled,
Till wi' their logic-jargon tired,
And in the depth of science mired,
To common sense they now appeal,
What wives and wabsters feel.

'Epistle to James Tennent'

But human bodies are sic fools,
For a' their colleges and schools,
That when nae real ills perplex them,
They mak enow themsel's to vex them.

'Twa Dogs'

Rank, Equality & Brotherhood

The cottage leaves the palace far behind;
What is a lordling's pomp? a cumbrous load,
Disguising oft the wretch of human kind,
Studied in arts of hell, in wickedness refined!

'The Cotter's Saturday Night'

For lords or kings I dinna mourn,
E'en let them die – for that they're born.

'Elegy on the Year 1788'

The poor, oppressèd, honest man
   Had never, sure, been born,
Had there not been some recompense
   To comfort those that mourn.

'Man was Made to Mourn'

If I'm designed yon lordling's slave,
   By Nature's law designed,
Why was an independent wish
   E'er planted in my mind?

Ibid.

A few seem favourites of fate,
   In pleasure's lap carest;
Yet, think not all the rich and great
   Are likewise truly blest:
But oh! what crowds in ev'ry land,
   All wretched and forlorn,
Thro' weary life this lesson learn
   That man was made to mourn.

Ibid.

The rank is but the guinea's stamp,
The man's the gowd for a' that.

'A Man's A Man For A' That'

Gie fools their silks, and knaves their wine,
A man's a man for a' that.
For a' that, an' a' that,
The honest man, tho' e'er sae poor,
Is king o' men for a' that.   *Ibid.*

A prince can mak a belted knight,
A marquis, duke, an' a' that!
But an honest man's aboon his might –
Gude faith, he mauna fa' that!   *Ibid.*

For a' that, an' a' that,
It's coming yet for a' that,
That man to man, the world o'er,
Shall brothers be for a' that.   *Ibid.*

We labour soon, we labour late,
To feed the titled knave, man;
And a' the comfort we're to get
Is that ayont the grave, man.

'The Tree of Liberty'

A country fellow at the pleugh,
His acre's tilled, he's right eneugh;
A country girl at her wheel,
Her dizzen's dune, she's unco weel;
But gentlemen, an' ladies warst,
Wi' ev'n-down want o' wark are curst.
They loiter, lounging, lank an' lazy;
Tho' deil-haet ails them, yet uneasy;
Their days insipid, dull an' tasteless;
Their nights unquiet, lang an' restless.

'Twa Dogs'

There's mony creditable stock
O' decent, honest, fawsont folk,
Are riven out baith root an' branch
Some rascal's pridefu' greed to quench.   *Ibid.*

One rank's as well's another …
For he but meets a brother.

'Lines on Meeting with Lord Daer'

If, in the vale of humble life,
The victim sad of fortune's strife,
I, thro' the tender-gushing tear,
Should recognise my master dear;
If friendless, low, we meet together,
Then, sir, your hand – my friend and brother!

'A Dedication'

O why should truest Worth and Genius pine
    Beneath the iron grasp of Want and Woe,
When titled knaves and idiot-greatness shine
    In all the splendour Fortune can bestow?

'Lines on Fergusson, the Poet'

There lives a lass beside yon park,
I'd rather hae her in her sark,
Than you wi' a' your thousand mark,
    That gars you look sae high.

'O Tibbie, I hae Seen the Day'

The peer I don't envy, I give him his bow;
I scorn not the peasant, tho' ever so low;
But a club of good fellows, like those that are here,
And a bottle like this, are my glory and care.

'No Churchman Am I'

Though I be poor, unnoticed, obscure,
My stomach's as proud as them a', man.

'The Ronalds of the Bennals'

The war'ly race may riches chase,
    An' riches still may fly them, O;
An' tho' at last they catch them fast,
    Their hearts can ne'er enjoy them, O.

'Green Grow the Rashes'

It's no in titles nor in rank:
It's no in wealth like Lon'on Bank,
    To purchase peace and rest.

'Epistle to Davie, a Brother Poet'

The war'ly race may drudge an' drive,
Hog-shouther, jundie, stretch, an' strive,
Let me fair Nature's face descrive,
      And I, wi' pleasure,
Shall let the busy, grumbling hive
      Bum owre their treasure.

'Epistle to William Simson'

Of Lordly acquaintance you boast,
      And the Dukes that you dined wi' yestreen;
Yet an insect's an insect at most,
      Tho' it crawl on the curl of a Queen!

'The Toad-Eater'

The warld's wealth, when I think on,
      Its pride and the lave o't;
My curse on silly coward man,
      That he should be the slave o't!

'Poortith Cauld and Restless Love'

How blest the wild-wood Indian's fate!
      He woos his artless dearie;
The silly bogles, wealth and state,
      Can never make him eerie.

Ibid.

The courtier cringes and bows,
      Ambition has likewise its plaything;
A coronet beams on his brows;
      And what is a coronet? – naething.

'Stanzas on Naething'

Now if ye're ane o' war'ly folk,
Wha rate the wearer by the cloak,
An' sklent on poverty their joke,
      Wi' bitter sneer,
Wi' you nae friendship I will troke,
      Nor cheap nor dear.

'To John Kennedy, Dumfries House'

Poor bodies hae naething but mowe.

'Why Should Na Poor Folk Mowe'

Wi' small to sell and less to buy,
Aboon distress, below envy,
O wha wad leave this humble state,
For a' the pride of a' the great?
Amid their flairing, idle toys,
Amid their cumbrous, dinsome joys,
Can they the peace and pleasure feel
Of Bessy at her spinnin-wheel?

'Bessy and her Spinnin-Wheel'

Should auld acquaintance be forgot,
    And never brought to mind?
Should auld acquaintance be forgot,
    And auld lang syne?

'Auld Lang Syne'

For auld lang syne, my dear,
    For auld lang syne,
We'll tak a cup o' kindness yet,
    For auld lang syne!   *Ibid.*

We twa hae run about the braes,
    And pou'd the gowans fine;
But we've wandered mony a weary fit,
    Sin' auld lang syne.   *Ibid.*

We twa hae paidled in the burn,
    Frae morning sun till dine;
But seas between us braid hae roared
    Sin' auld lang syne.   *Ibid.*

And there's a hand my trusty frere!
    And gie's a hand o' thine!
And we'll tak' a right gude-willie waught,
    For auld lang syne.   *Ibid.*

Devil take the life of reaping the fruits that another must eat.

Letter to Mrs Dunlop, 24 September 1792

Love

O my luve is like a red, red rose
   That's newly sprung in June:
O my luve is like the melodie,
   That's sweetly played in tune.

'A Red, Red Rose'

'Till a' the seas gang dry, my dear,
   And the rocks melt wi' the sun;
And I will luve thee still, my dear,
   While the sands o' life shall run.   *Ibid.*

Had we never loved sae kindly,
Had we never loved sae blindly,
Never met – or never parted -
We had ne'er been broken hearted.

'Ae Fond Kiss'

Love thou hast pleasures, and deep hae I loved;
Love thou hast sorrows, and sair hae I proved;
But this bruised heart that now bleeds in my breast,
I can feel by its throbbings, will soon be at rest.

'The Tear-Drop'

O kissin is the key o' luve,
And clappin is the lock.   'O Can Ye Labour Lea?'

What is life when wanting Love?
   Night without a morning.
Love's the cloudless summer sun,
   Nature gay adorning.

'Thine Am I, My Faithful Fair'

If to love thy heart denies,
Oh, in pity hide the sentence
Under friendship's kind disguise!

'Thou Fair Eliza'

Talk not of love, it gives me pain,
   For love has been my foe;
He bound me in an iron chain,
   And plunged me deep in woe.

'Love in the Guise of Friendship'

The scenes where wretched Fancy roves,
Pursuing past, unhappy loves.

'Farewell Song to the Banks of Ayr'

A gaudy dress and gentle air
   May slightly touch the heart;
But it's innocence and modesty
   That polishes the dart.

'Handsome Nell'

For the man that loves his mistress well,
Nae travel makes him weary.

'Here's to Thy Health'

I lo'e the dear lassie because she lo'es me.

'You Wild Mossy Mountains'

Slighted love is sair to bide.

'Duncan Gray'

O luve will venture in where wisdom ance has
been.

'The Posie'

Wi' lightsome heart I pu'd a rose,
   Fu' sweet upon its thorny tree!
And my fause luver staw my rose,
   But ah! he left the thorn wi' me.

'The Banks O' Doon'

To see her is to love her,
And love but her for ever;
For Nature made her what she is,
And never made anither!

'Bonnie Lesley'

The tender thrill, the pitying tear,
The generous purpose noble dear,
The gentle look that rage disarms –
These are all immortal charms.

'My Peggy's Charms'

Even Wedlock asks not love beyond
    Death's tie-dissolving portal;
But thou, omnipotently fond,
    May'st promise love immortal!

'To Alex. Cunningham'

Who can trace
The process of bewitching?

Ibid.

As little recked I sorrow's power,
    Until the flowery snare
O' witching Love, in luckless hour,
    Made me the thrall o' care.

'Now Spring Has Clad'

My life was ance that careless stream,
    That wanton trout was I;
But Love, wi' unrelenting beam,
    Has scorched my fountains dry.

Ibid.

All in its rude and prickly bower,
    That crimson rose, how sweet and fair;
But love is still a sweeter flower,
    Amid life's thorny path o' care.

'O Bonie was Yon Rosy Brier'

In Love's delightful fetters she chains the willing soul!

'Mark Yonder Pomp of Costly Fashion'

Tho' a' my daily care thou art,
    And a' my nightly dream,
I'll hide the struggle in my heart,
    And say it is esteem.

'Esteem for Chloris'

Grace, beauty, and elegance fetter her lover,
And maidenly modesty fixes the chain.

'Lovely Young Jessie'

O why should Fate sic pleasure have,
    Life's dearest bands untwining?
Or why sae sweet a flower as love
    Depend on Fortune's shining?

'Poortith Cauld and Restless Love'

She's fresh as the morning, the fairest in May;
She's sweet as the evening amang the new hay;
As blythe and as artless as the lambs on the lea,
And dear to my heart as the light to my e'e.

'Auld Rob Morris'

The warld's wrack, we share o't,
The warstle and the care o't;
Wi' her I'll blythely bear it,
    And think my lot divine.

'My Wife's a Winsome Wee Thing'

Ye monarchs, take the East and West
    Frae Indus to Savannah;
Gie me, within my straining grasp,
    The melting form of Anna.
There I'll despise Imperial charms,
    An Empress or Sultana,
While dying raptures in her arms
    I give and take wi' Anna!

'The Gowden Locks of Anna'

First when Maggie was my care,
    Heaven, I thought, was in her air,
Now we're married – speir nae mair,
    But whistle o'er the lave o't!

'Whistle O'er the Lave O't'

The captive bands may chain the hands,
But love enslaves the man.

'Beware O' Bonie Ann'

Content am I, if heaven shall give
    But happiness to thee;
And as wi' thee I wish to live,
    For thee I'll bear to die.

'It Is Na, Jean, Thy Bonie Face'

Something, in ilka part o' thee,
    To praise, to love, I find,
But dear as is thy form to me,
    Still dearer is thy mind.

Ibid.

The lover may sparkle and glow
    Approaching his bonie bit gay thing:
But marriage will soon let him know
    He's gotten – a buskit-up naething.

'Stanzas on Naething'

'Twas na her bonie blue e'e was my ruin,
Fair though she be, that was ne'er my undoin';
'Twas the dear smile when naebody did mind us,
'Twas the bewitching, sweet, stown glance o'
    kindness.

' 'Twas Na her Bonie Blue E'e'

It ne'er was wealth, it ne'er was wealth,
    That coft contentment, peace, or pleasure:
The bands and bliss o' mutual love,
    O that's the chiefest warld's treasure.

'Braw Lads O' Galla Water'

If Heaven a draught of heavenly pleasure spare,
One cordial in this melancholy vale,
    'Tis when a youthful, loving, modest pair
In other's arms, breathe out the tender tale,
Beneath the milk-white thorn that scents the ev'ning gale.

'The Cotter's Saturday Night'

If anything on earth deserves the name of rapture or
transport, it is the feelings of green eighteen, in the
company of the mistress of his heart.

Journal, April 1793

Youth, Age & Death

Nae man can tether Time nor Tide.

'Tam O'Shanter'

A few days may – a few years must –
Repose us in the silent dust.

'Sketch – New Year's Day'

Life is but a day at most,
Sprung from night, in darkness lost;
Hope not sunshine every hour,
Fear not clouds will always lour.

'Written in Friars' Carse Hermitage'

As the shades of evening close,
Beckoning thee to long repose;
As life itself becomes disease,
Seek the chimney-nook of ease;
There ruminate with sober thought,
On all thou'st seen, and heard, and wrought,
And teach the sportive younkers round,
Saws of experience, sage and sound.   *Ibid.*

O man! while in thy early years
    How prodigal of time!
Mis-spending all thy precious hours -
    Thy glorious, youthful prime!

'Man was Made to Mourn'

O Death! the poor man's dearest friend,
    The kindest and the best!
Welcome the hour my aged limbs
    Are laid with thee at rest!
The great, the wealthy fear thy blow,
    From pomp and pleasure torn;
But oh! a blest relief for those
    That weary-laden mourn.   *Ibid.*

Hale be your heart, hale be your fiddle,
Lang may your elbuck jink an' diddle,
To cheer you through the weary widdle
    O' war'ly cares;
Till bairns' bairns kindly cuddle
    Your auld grey hairs.   'Second Epistle to Davie'

O Life! how pleasant in the morning,
Young Fancy's rays the hills adorning!
Cold-pausing Caution's lesson scorning,
    We frisk away,
Like school-boys, at th' expected warning,
    To joy an' play.   'Epistle to James Smith'

Oh, Age has weary days,
    And nights o' sleepless pain:
Thou golden time o' youthfu' prime,
    Why comes thou not again?   'The Winter of Life'

When Death's dark stream I ferry o'er,
    (A time that surely shall come),
In Heav'n itself I'll ask no more,
    Than just a Highland welcome.

                  'Epigram on Parting'

I can die – but canna part.
           'Ca' the Yowes to the Knowes'

Now farewell light, thou sunshine bright,
    And all beneath the sky!
May coward shame disdain his name,
    The wretch that dare not die!

                'M'Pherson's Farewell'

O pale, pale now, those rosy lips,
    I aft hae kissed sae fondly!
And closed for aye, the sparkling glance
    That dwelt on me sae kindly!
And mouldering now in silent dust,
    That heart that lo'ed me dearly!
But still within my bosom's care
    Shall live my Highland Mary.   'Highland Mary'

Below thir stanes lie James's banes;
   O Death, it's my opinion,
Thou ne'er took such a bleth'rin bitch
   Into thy dark dominion!

'Epitaph on a Noisy Polemic'

Whoe'er thou art, O, reader, know
   That Death has murdered Johnie;
An' here his *body* lies fu' low;
   For *soul* he ne'er had ony.

'Epitaph on Wee Johnie'

If there's another world, he lives in bliss;
If there is none, he made the best of this.

'Epitaph on my own Friend'

Ye little know the ills ye court,
   When manhood is your wish!
The losses, the crosses,
   That active man enrage;
The fears all, the tears all,
   Of dim declining Age!

'Despondency – an Ode'

What a transient business is life! Very lately I was a boy;
but t'other day I was a young man; and I already begin
to feel the rigid fibre and stiffening joints of old age
coming fast o'er my frame.

Letter to Mrs Dunlop, 29 December 1795

Happiness & Consolations

Happy! ye sons of busy life,
Who, equal to the bustling strife,
  No other view regard.

'Despondency – An Ode'

How blest the Solitary's lot,
Who, all-forgetting, all-forgot,
  Within his humble cell –
The cavern wild with tangling roots –
  Beside his crystal well.   *Ibid.*

Let Prudence bless Enjoyment's Cup,
Then raptured sip and sip it up.

'Written in Friars' Carse Hermitage'

Happiness is but a name,
Make Content and Ease thy aim.

Ibid.

Ambition is a meteor gleam,
Fame a restless, airy dream;
Pleasures insects on the wing
Round Peace, the tenderest flower of spring.

Ibid.

For the Future be prepared,
Guard, wherever thou canst guard,
But thy utmost duty done,
Welcome what thou canst not shun.

Ibid.

Those that sip the dew alone,
Make the butterflies thy own;
Those that would the bloom devour,
Crush the locusts, save the flower.

Ibid.

Where are the joys I have met in the morning?
> 'Where are the Joys'

But first, before you see heaven's glory,
May ye get mony a merry story,
Mony a laugh, and mony a drink,
And aye eneugh o' needfu' clink.
> 'Epistle to James Tennent'

If happiness hae not her seat
   An' centre in the breast,
We may be wise, or rich, or great,
   But never can be blest;
Nae treasures nor pleasures
   Could make us happy lang;
The heart's aye's the part aye
   That makes us right or wrang.
> 'Epistle to Davie, a Brother Poet'

Then let us cheefu' acquiesce,
Nor make our scanty pleasures less,
   By pining at our state.   *Ibid.*

Love blinks, Wit slaps, an' social Mirth
Forgets there's Care upo' the earth.   'Twa Dogs'

Your darkest terrors may be vain,
Your brightest hopes may fail.
> 'Ode on the Departed Regency Bill'

What is title, what is treasure,
   What is reputation's care?
If we lead a life of pleasure,
   'Tis no matter how or where!
> 'The Jolly Beggars'

This life, sae far's I understand,
Is a' enchanted fairy-land,
Where Pleasure is the magic-wand,
   That, wielded right,
Make hours like minutes, hand in hand,
   Dance by fu' light.   'Epistle to James Smith'

We wander there, we wander here,
We eye the rose upon the brier,
Unmindful that the thorn is near,
    Among the leaves;
And tho' the puny would appear,
    Short while it grieves.

Ibid.

Gie wealth to some be-ledgered cit,
    In cent. per cent.;
But give me real, sterling wit,
    And I'm content.   *Ibid.*

An anxious e'e I never throws
Behind my lug, or by my nose;
I jouk beneath Misfortune's blows
    As weel's I may;
Sworn foe to sorrow, care, and prose,
    I rhyme away.

Ibid.

O Dulness! portion of the truly blest!
Calm sheltered haven of eternal rest!
Thy sons ne'er madden in the fierce extremes
Of Fortune's polar frost, or torrid beams.

'Second Epistle to Robert Graham'

Some have meat and cannot eat.
    Some cannot eat that want it:
But we have meat and we can eat,
    Sae let the Lord be thankit.

'Burns Grace at Kirkcudbright'

So much laughter, so much life enjoyed.

'Address'

To sum up all, be merry, I advise;
And as we're merry, may we still be wise.

Ibid.

Every new work is a new spring of joy.

'The Whistle'

But gie me a cannie hour at e'en,
    My arms about my dearie, O;
An' war'ly cares, an' war'ly men,
    May a'gae tapsalteerie, O!

'Green Grow the Rashes'

There's nought but care on ev'ry han',
    In ev'ry hour that passes, O:
What signifies the life o' man,
    An 'twere na for the lasses, O.

Ibid.

Then catch the moments as they fly,
    And use them as ye ought, man:
Believe me, happiness is shy,
    And comes not aye when sought, man.

'A Bottle and a Friend'

Tho' by the bye, abroad why will you roam?
Good sense and taste are natives here at home.

'Prologue Spoken at the Theatre of Dumfries'

Go on, sweet bird, and soothe my care,
Thy tuneful notes will hush despair.

'Go On, Sweet Bird'

May still your life from day to day,
Nae *lento largo* in the play,
But *allegretto forte* gay,
    Harmonious flow,
A sweeping, kindling, bauld strathspey -
    Encore! Bravo!

'Epistle to Major Logan'

We've faults and failings – granted clearly,
We're frail backsliding mortals merely;
Eve's bonie squad, priests wyte them sheerly
    For our grand fa';
But still, but still – I like them dearly;
    God bless them a'!

Ibid.

My partner in the merry core,
    She roused the forming strain;
I see her yet, the sonsie quean,
    That lighted up my jingle,
Her witching smile, her pawky een
    That gart my heart-strings tingle.

'Epistle to Mrs Scott'

Ye Pow'rs wha mak mankind your care,
And dish them out their bill o' fare,
Auld Scotland wants nae skinking ware
    That jaups in luggies;
But, if ye wish her gratefu' prayer,
    Gie her a haggis!

'Address to a Haggis'

The greybeard, old Wisdom, may boast of his
    treasures;
    Give me with gay Folly to live;
I grant him his calm-blooded, time-settled
    pleasures,
    But Folly has raptures to give.

'The Raptures of Folly'

Reader, attend! whether thy soul
Soars fancy's flights beyond the pole,
Or darkling grubs this earthly hole,
    In low pursuit:
Know, prudent, cautious, self-control
    Is wisdom's root.

'A Bard's Epitaph'

Then sore harassed, and tired at last, with Fortune's
                                vain delusion, O,
I dropped my schemes, like idle dreams, and came to
                                this conclusion, O –
The past was bad, and the future hid, its good or ill
                                untrièd, O,
But the present hour was in my pow'r, and so I would
                                enjoy it, O.

'My Father was a Farmer'

Men, Women & Mankind

You'll find mankind an unco squad.

'Epistle to a Young Friend'

From ev'ry joy and pleasure torn,
Life's weary vale I'll wander thro';
    And hopeless, comfortless, I'll mourn
A faithless woman's broken vow!

'The Lament'

Ah, gentle dames! it gars me greet,
To think how mony counsels sweet,
How mony lengthened, sage advices,
The husband frae the wife despises!

'Tam O'Shanter'

To grant a heart is fairly civil,
But to grant a maidenhead's the devil.

'Epistle to James Tennent'

To make a happy fireside clime
    To weans and wife,
That's the true pathos and sublime
    Of human life.

Ibid.

But how capricious are mankind,
    Now loathing, now desirous!
We married men, how oft we find
    The best of things will tire us!

'On Marriage'

An auld wife's tongue a feckless matter
To gie ane fash.

'A Poet's Welcome to his Love-Begotten Daughter'

The billows on the ocean,
The breezes idly roaming,
The cloud's uncertain motion,
They are but types of Woman.

'Deluded Swain, the Pleasure'

Mankind are his show-box – a friend, would you
know him?
Pull the string, Ruling Passion – the picture will
show him.

'Sketch in Verse'

In spite of his fine theoretic positions,
Mankind is a science defies definitions.

Ibid.

Such is the flaw, or the depth of the plan,
In the make of that wonderful creature called Man,
No two virtues, whatever relation they claim,
Nor even two different shades of the same,
Though like as ever twin brother to brother,
Possessing the one shall imply you've the other.

Ibid.

I have been a Deevil the feck o' my life …
But ne'er was in hell till I met wi' a wife.

'Kelly Burn Braes'

The gust o' joy, the balm of woe,
The saul o' life, the heaven below,
Is rapture-giving woman.

'Epistle to Mrs Scott'

I've nane in female servant station,
(Lord keep me aye frae a' temptation!)
I hae nae wife – and that my bliss is,
An ye have laid nae tax on misses.

'The Inventory'

Silly woman has her warlike arts,
Her tongue and eyes – her dreaded spear and darts.

'Second Epistle to Robert Graham'

True it is, she had one failing;
Had ae woman ever less?

'The Celebrated Miss Burns'

An armful o' luve is her bosom sae plump,
A span o' delight is her middle sae jump;
A taper, white leg, and a thumpin thie,
And a fiddle near by, an ye play a wee!

'Muirland Meg'

I maun hae a wife, whatsoe'er she be;
An she be a woman, that's enough for me.
If she be bony, I shall think her right:
If that she be ugly, where's the odds at night?
O, an she be young, how happy shall I be!
If that she be auld, the sooner she will die.
If that she be fruitfu', O! what a joy is there!
If she should be barren, less will be my care.
If she like a drappie, she and I'll agree;
If she dinna like it, there's the mair for me.
Be she green or gray; be she black or fair;
Let her be a woman, I shall seek nae mair.

'Broom Besoms'

A bonie lass, I will confess,
    Is pleasant to the e'e;
But without some better qualities
    She's no a lass for me.   'Handsome Nell'

Farewell dear, deluding Woman,
The joy of joys!

'Epistle to James Smith'

Want only of wisdom denied her respect,
Want only of goodness denied her esteem.

'Monody'

I murder hate by flood or field,
    Tho' glory's name may screen us;
In wars at hame I'll spend my blood -
    Life-giving wars of Venus.

'I Murder Hate'

Cursed be the man, the poorest wretch in life,
The crouching vassal to a tyrant wife!

'The Hen-Pecked Husband'

As father Adam first was fooled,
　　A case that's still too common,
Here lies a man a woman ruled –
　　The Devil ruled the woman.

'Epitaph on a Henpecked Squire'

Awa' wi' your witchcraft o' Beauty's alarms,
The slender bit Beauty you grasp in your arms,
O, gie me the lass that has acres o' charms!
O, gie me the lass wi' the well-stockit farms!

'A Lass Wi' A Tocher'

Ne'er break your heart for ae rebuke,
　　But think upon it still, jo:
That gin the lassie winna do't,
　　Ye'll find anither will, jo.

'O Steer Her Up An' Haud Her Gaun'

On peace an' rest my hand was bent,
　　And, fool I was! I married;
But never honest man's intent
　　Sae cursedly miscarried.

'O Aye My Wife She Dang Me'

A man may drink, and no be drunk;
　　A man may fight, and no be slain;
A man may kiss a bonie lass,
　　And aye be welcome back again!

'Duncan Davison'

Kindness, sweet kindness, in the fond-sparkling e'e,
Has lustre outshining the diamond to me.

'You Wild Mossy Mountains'

It's not her air, her form, her face,
　　Tho' matching beauty's fabled queen;
'Tis her mind that shines in every grace,
　　An' chiefly her roguish een.

'The Lass of Cessnock Banks'

Poetry & Criticism

Pity the best of words should be but wind!

'Epistle to Robert Graham'

(Nature may have her whim as well as we:
Her Hogarth-art, perhaps she meant to show it),
She forms the thing and christens it – a Poet …
A mortal quite unfit for Fortune's strife,
Yet oft the sport of all the ills of life;
Prone to enjoy each pleasure riches give,
Yet haply wanting wherewithal to life;
Longing to wipe each tear, to heal each groan,
Yet frequent all unheeded in his own.

Ibid.

If these mortals, the critics, should bustle,
I care not, not I – let the critics go whistle.

'Sketch in Verse'

The muse, nae poet ever fand her,
Till by himself he learned to wander,
Adown some trottin burn's meander
   An' no think lang:
O sweet to stray, an' pensive ponder
   A heart-felt sang!

'Epistle to William Simson'

Critics – appalled, I venture on the name;
Those cut-throat bandits in the paths of fame:
Bloody dissectors, worse than ten Munroes,
He hacks to teach, they mangle to expose.

'Second Epistle to Robert Graham'

Our friends, the Reviewers,
Those chippers and hewers,
Are judges of mortar and stone, sir;
  But of meet and unmeet,
  In a fabric complete,
I'll boldly pronounce they are none, sir.

'Impromptu Lines to Captain Riddell'

Some rhyme a neebor's name to lash;
Some rhyme (vain thought!) for needfu' cash;
Some rhyme to court the country clash,
  An' raise a din;
For me, an aim I never fash;
  I rhyme for fun.

'Epistle to James Smith'

The simple Bard unbroke by rules of art,
He pours the wild effusions of the heart;
And if inspired, 'tis Nature's powers inspire,
Hers all the melting thrill, hers the kindling fire.

'Motto Prefixed to the Author's First Publication'

Ne'er scorn a poor Poet like me,
  For idly just living and breathing,
While people of every degree
  Are busy employed about – naething.

'Stanzas on Naething'

That Bards are second-sighted is nae joke,
And ken the lingo of the spiritual folk;
Fays, Spunkies, Kelpies, a', they can explain them,
And even the very diels they brawly ken them.

'The Brigs of Ayr'

I lo'e her mysel, but darena weel tell,
  My poverty keeps me in awe, man;
For making o' rhymes, and working at times,
  Does little or naething at a', man.

'The Ronalds of the Bennals'

Glossary

aboon, above
a-gley, awry
ayont, beyond

ba', ball
bogle, demon
braw, handsome
bree, brew
breeks, breeches
brunstane, brimstone
bum, hum
busk, dress

callan, youth
canty, cheerful
carlin, old woman
chiel, lad
clachan, hamlet
clap, caress
clink, money
coft, bought
coggie, vessel, womb
coof, fool
crabbit, ill-natured

daffin, frolic
daur, care
deil-haet, devil take it
diddle, jig
dight, clean
ding, overcome, be worn out
dizzen, dozen
doited, senile
dool, sorrow
downa, cannot
doytin, stumbling around
drant, sulk
drumlie, muddy

een, eyes
elbuck, elbow

fash, trouble
fause, false
fawsont, decent
feck, greater portion
fou, full, drunk

gang, go
gar, cause, compel
gear, wealth, money
gin, if, whether
gleg, sharp, clever
gowan, daisy
gowd, gold
grat, wept
gude-willie, generous

hirple, limp
hoast, cough
houghmagandie, fornication
hurdies, buttocks

ilka, each, every

jaup, splash
jo, sweetheart
jundie, shove aside

keek, peep
kittle, tickle
knappin-hammer, hammer for breaking stones

laigh, low
lallans, lowland language
lear, lore
leeze me on, I am happy in
looves, palms
luggies, small dishes

maukin, hare
maun, must
melvie, soil with mud
mowe, make love
mutchkin, English pint

nappy, strong ale
neist, next

pang, cram
plack, small coin
pou, pull

puir, poor

remead, remedy
rowth, abundance

sair, sore, to serve
sark, chemise
scrieve, glide along
shools, shovels
sklent, aslant
skouth, scope
sonsie, buxom
staw, stole
steek, shut, enclose
stirk, young bullock
stoup, tankard
strathspey, a dance
styme, glimmer
syne, since, then

tapsalteerie, topsy-turvy
thir, these
tocher, dowry
troke, exchange

unco, uncommon, very
usquabae, whisky

wabster, weaver
waesucks, alas
wale, choice
wame, belly, womb
war'ly, worldly
weans, children
widdle, trouble
whittle, knife
whunstane, whinstone
wight, fellow
winnock, window
wrack, rubbish, possessions
wud, angry
wyte, blame

yill, ale
younkers, youngsters
yowes, ewes